The American Alligator

by Steve Potts

Content Consultant:
Joe Schaeffer, Associate Professor
Department of Wildlife, Ecology, and
Conservation
University of Florida

C A P S T O N E   P R E S S
M A N K A T O ,   M I N N E S O T A

C A P S T O N E   P R E S S

818 North Willow Street • Mankato, Minnesota 56001
http://www.capstone-press.com

Printed in the United States of America.

Library of Congress Cataloging-in-Publication Data
Potts, Steve, 1956-
   The American alligator/by Steve Potts.
   p. cm.--(Wildlife in North America)
   Includes bibliographical references (p.45) and index.
   Summary: Describes the characteristics, habitats, and life cycle of the American alligator.
   ISBN 1-56065-581-X
   1. American alligator--Juvenile literature. [1. Alligators]
I. Title.   II. Series.
QL666.C925P686   1997
597.98--dc21

                                               97-19646
                                                  CIP
                                                      AC

Photo credits
William H. Allen, Jr., 6, 36
William Muñoz, 14, 22, 30, 32, 39
Nature Images/Helen Longest-Slaughter, 21
Rick Poley, cover, 12, 18
Laura Riley, 8, 24
James H. Robinson, 10, 16, 26, 35, 29, 42-43
Unicorn Stock/Doris Brookes, 41

Table of Contents

Fast Facts about American Alligators

Scientific Name: *Alligator mississippiensis*

Length: An average male alligator grows to about 12 feet (360 centimeters) long. The average female is shorter. It grows to about eight feet (240 centimeters) long.

Weight: An average male alligator weighs up to 500 pounds (225 kilograms). A female alligator generally weighs up to 250 pounds (113 kilograms).

Life span: In the wild, alligators live from 20 to 30 years.

Habits: When water levels are low, an alligator digs a gator hole and lives in it.

Color: Adult alligators are grayish-black. Their undersides are light yellow. Young alligators are also grayish-black with yellow bands and spots.

Food: Alligators eat almost anything. They eat fish, crabs, crayfish, snails, turtles, muskrats, snakes, snails, and birds.

Reproduction: The alligator mating season begins in April. Three weeks later, the female lays 20 to 50 eggs. The eggs hatch in two months.

Range: American alligators live in the southeastern United States. They are found in Alabama, Arkansas, North Carolina, South Carolina, Florida, Georgia, Louisiana, Mississippi, Oklahoma, and Texas.

Habitat: Alligators live in swamps and wetlands. They also live in lakes and small bodies of water.

State Symbols: The alligator is the official state reptile for Florida and Louisiana.

Chapter 1

The American Alligator

The American alligator has lived through many hardships. It is one of only three living members of the crocodilian family. A family is a group of related animals. Crocodiles and caimans are the other two members of the crocodilian family. Dinosaurs were members of the crocodilian family, but they became extinct. Extinct means that something has died out and no longer exists.

The alligator almost died out as well. But it is no longer in danger of extinction. Today,

The alligator is a member of the crocodilian family.

Many teeth stick out when crocodiles close their mouths.

alligators only live in the southeastern United States. They live in swamps or wetlands.

Reptiles

Alligators are reptiles. A reptile is a cold-blooded animal. This means the temperature of a reptile's body changes depending on the weather. In cold weather, their bodies cool down. In warm weather, their bodies heat up. Alligators would die in areas that are too cold or too hot. They can also change their body temperatures by moving into warm, sunny areas or cool, deep water areas.

Reptiles have other features, too. They have backbones. They also lay eggs on dry land.

Alligators and Crocodiles

Some people confuse alligators with crocodiles. The two reptiles look a lot alike. But there are two main differences.

The first difference is in where they live. Nearly all alligators live in fresh water. Many crocodiles live in salt water.

The second difference is in how they look. Alligators are mostly grayish-black, but crocodiles are mostly light brown. Alligators have a wider snout than crocodiles. A snout is the long front part of an animal's head. The nose, mouth, and jaws are part of the snout. When alligators close their mouths, people cannot see many bottom teeth. People can see many teeth when crocodiles close their mouths.

On land, alligators can run as fast as a person.

Appearance

The name alligator comes from the Spanish term el lagarto. This means the lizard. Spanish explorers thought the alligator looked like a giant lizard. In some ways, this is true. An alligator's body is slightly rounded. It has short legs, so its body stays close to the ground.

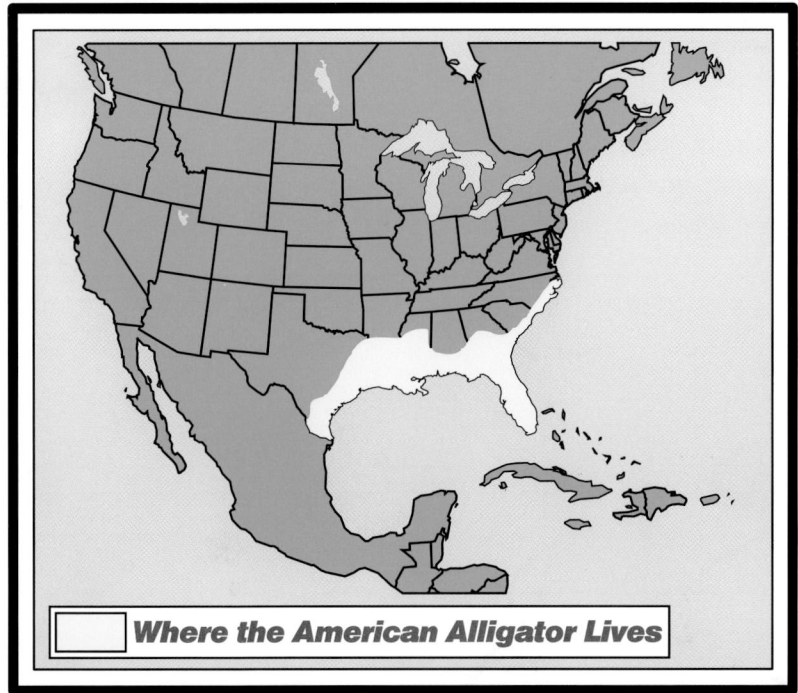

Where the American Alligator Lives

Male alligators grow to about 12 feet (360 centimeters) long. Female alligators are shorter. They grow to about eight feet (240 centimeters) long.

An alligator's head is wide. Its eyes and nostrils stick up higher than the rest of its head. This way an alligator can see and breathe even if the rest of its body is underwater.

An alligator has four short legs. The two back legs are slightly longer than the front ones. Alligator legs may be short, but they

Alligators use their jaws to crush and kill their prey.

have powerful muscles. On land, alligators can run as fast as a person for short distances.

Alligators' front feet have five toes that are topped by sharp claws. Alligators' back feet have only four toes. On each back foot, they have a little stump of bone instead of a fifth toe. Each toe also has a claw. Their back feet are webbed, too. This means that a flap of skin grows between two toes. Webbed feet help alligators swim.

Jaws

Jaws are important to an alligator. An alligator uses its jaws to crush and kill prey. Prey are animals that are hunted and eaten for food. An alligator's lower jaw is its deadliest part. It is controlled by strong muscles. It can close with enough strength to snap off a human leg. The upper part of an alligator's jaw does not move.

An alligator has 80 teeth. There are 40 teeth on the upper jaw and 40 teeth on the lower jaw. An alligator has both large and small teeth. The largest teeth can grow to be about three inches (eight centimeters) long.

Alligator teeth last about one year. Then new teeth grow in to replace the old ones. Young alligators lose many old teeth and grow many new teeth. This process stops when alligators grow older. Some older alligators have very few teeth. An alligator goes through 2,000 to 3,000 teeth in its lifetime.

Tail and Skin

An alligator has a long tail that is about half as long as its body. Its tail muscles help it swim as fast as six miles (10 kilometers) an hour. An

alligator can swim faster than some motorboats. An alligator's tail is special in another way, too. It will grow a new tail if parts of it are cut off.

Adult alligators are grayish-black on top. Their undersides are lighter. An alligator's skin is rough and thick. It is covered with scales that have scutes inside them. Scutes are small, round discs of bone. Bony plates protect an alligator's body and tail. In fact, an alligator's hide is almost as strong as metal armor. The hide helps keep an alligator from getting seriously injured when it fights during mating season.

Alligators in Water

Alligators are well suited to being underwater. But alligators breathe air, so they must swim to the surface of the water to breathe. They can stay underwater without breathing for more than an hour.

Alligators can dive underwater quickly to escape from danger. Special flaps of skin protect their ears, throats, and noses. These flaps close when alligators dive. The flaps seal out water.

Three eyelids help protect an alligator's sensitive eyes. Like humans, an alligator has an upper and a lower eyelid. Unlike humans, an alligator also has a special third eyelid. The third eyelid protects its eyes when it swims underwater. An alligator can see through this eyelid and keep its eyes dry.

Chapter 2

Survival

Whe an alligator becomes an adult, it chooses a territory. It fights other adult alligators that enter the territory. When many alligators occupy a small space, they sometimes fight over land. Fights over territories are often bloody and fierce.

Gator Holes

Sometimes there are no large bodies of water by an alligator's territory. Then it digs a hole deep enough until it fills with water. The hole is commonly called a gator hole.

Each alligator chooses a place in a swamp or wetland for its gator holes. Some choose areas

Adult alligators choose a territory.

near river banks. The soil in these places is soft. Water lies close to the surface. Alligators use their noses, tails, and feet to dig deep holes in the soft ground. They dig until water starts filling their holes. Gator holes can be up to 15 feet (four and one-half meters) deep and 30 feet (nine meters) wide. It usually takes many years for alligators to finish digging their holes.

When alligators are finished digging, gator holes often look like small ponds. If the gator hole is large enough, it may also be home to fish, turtles, and birds. Other animals might drink there, too. Most gator holes are deep enough to hold water during dry periods. The gator holes help keep these other animals alive during dry periods. In an important way, the alligators help preserve animal life in swamps.

An alligator usually lives alone in its gator hole. It often spends its entire life in the same gator hole. Sometimes an older alligator will allow young alligators to live in the same gator hole. But when the young alligators grow older, they must find their own territories.

Much of an alligator's life is spent in its gator hole. It keeps the hole clean of plants and soil. This keeps the water clean for swimming.

Dens

Some alligators build dens in river banks or by their gator holes. Sometimes alligators use small caves with underwater entrances as their dens. Other alligators dig their dens. First, they tunnel

from the water into the soil. The tunnels can be as long as 20 feet (six meters). Then at the end of the tunnels, they dig little rooms above the water level. These rooms are the dens.

Alligators live in their dens during dry seasons. They also stay in their dens if the weather becomes too cold. Because alligators are cold-blooded, they are not active in cold weather. Instead, they rest in their dens.

Alligators that live in lakes usually do not build dens. If ice forms on the water, they use their bodies to break holes in the ice. That way they can breathe.

Staying in Territories

Both young and old alligators like to stay close to their territories. Some scientists have taken alligators out of their gator holes. They put radio collars around the alligators' necks. This helped the scientists keep track of the alligators' movements.

The scientists drove the alligators far away from their gator holes. Then they released the alligators. Some of the alligators walked and

swam more than 20 miles (35 kilometers) to return to their homes.

Food

Alligators will eat almost anything. When they are young, alligators eat insects, small fish, crabs, crayfish, and snails.

Adult alligators eat turtles, muskrats, snakes, fish, snails, and birds. Alligators also

eat carrion. Carrion is the flesh of dead animals. Occasionally, alligators will eat each other.

In many parts of the southeastern United States, alligators help to control rodents. They eat rats and mice that come within their reach. If given the chance, alligators will even eat small pets such as dogs and cats.

In summer, adult alligators eat about 20 pounds (nine kilograms) of food every week. They do not eat much food in winter because it is cold. In the cold, alligators are inactive. Alligators can live without food for more than three months at a time.

Hunting for Food

Alligators do most of their hunting at night. They have several small organs on each side of their snout. These organs help alligators smell and find food.

Once an alligator smells food, it hunts. An alligator will often swim or float with its entire body underwater. It keeps only its nostrils and eyes above the water. Then it swims silently

An alligator often floats with its entire body underwater.

An alligator's skin helps it blend into its surroundings.

toward its target. Once it is close enough, the alligator suddenly raises its head out of the water and attacks its prey.

Other times, an alligator swims beneath ducks and other animals that are swimming on the water. Once the alligator is directly below the animal, the alligator swims upward and tries to swallow it. An alligator also might grab large prey like deer and pull them underwater. The large prey die by drowning.

An alligator's grayish-black skin helps it blend into its surroundings. Many prey animals do not notice the alligator. Sometimes an alligator will hunt by floating quietly on the water. When an animal or fish swims close, the alligator quickly attacks its prey.

Eating

An alligator cannot chew even though it has many sharp teeth. It uses its teeth to kill and tear chunks from its prey. An alligator swallows these chunks whole.

An alligator's tongue is fastened to the bottom of its mouth. Its tongue barely moves. Because of this, an alligator cannot swallow its food like a human. An alligator must tilt its head upward. The food falls down its throat and into its stomach.

Sometimes alligators swallow hard objects like pieces of wood. These objects are called gastroliths. Scientists believe gastroliths help alligators grind and digest their food.

ALLIGATOR TRACKS

FRONT FOOT BACK FOOT

An Alligator's Life

Many people see alligators basking. Basking means sitting in the sun. The sun gives alligators needed body heat on cool days.

Alligators do not sit in the sun all day. They would become too hot. Alligators can choose between three different ways to cool themselves. First, they can swim. Second, they can move into the shade. Third, they can open their mouths. When fresh air blows inside their mouths, it helps to cool them down. This

Sometimes alligators open their mouths to cool down.

works just like when air blows over people's wet skin.

Communication

Alligators display different behaviors that send messages to other alligators. Sometimes an alligator arches its back. It raises its head and tail out of the water, too. This can mean either come closer or leave. Other alligators know which way to interpret the behavior.

Alligators also hiss. The hiss tells people and other alligators to leave them alone. Other times, alligators gather air in their throats to bellow. A bellow is like a loud roar. Scientists think one reason male alligators bellow is to attract females during mating season.

Young alligators croak when they are scared. These calls attract their mothers. The mothers may or may not defend their young.

Mating

Mating season starts in April. Alligators are at least six feet (180 centimeters) long when they mate. It takes them about 10 years to grow this long. Alligators mate once a year. They have only

Alligators gather air in their throats to bellow.

one mating partner each year. Sometimes males want to mate with the same females. Then they fight over the females.

During courtship, the male may follow the female wherever she goes. He might wait two weeks before she agrees to mate. In the water, he blows bubbles around the female. They play chasing games. Finally, they mate.

Once the alligators have mated, the male leaves. The female alligator looks for a place to build a nest.

Alligator Nest

The female usually builds the nest close to her gator hole. She chooses a place 10 to 15 feet (three to four and one-half meters) away from the water. This is so the nest will not flood if the water rises. She often chooses a shady spot under bushes or trees.

The female uses plants, leaves, mud, and small branches to make the nest. If those materials are not available, she uses whatever is nearby. She might use sand or grass. Sometimes females begin building nests but do not finish. They might start building two or three nests before they decide to use one.

A finished nest is large and shaped like a cone. Most nests are three feet (90 centimeters) high and four to six feet (120 to 180 centimeters) wide on the bottom. The female alligator crawls over the nest to press down the surface. Once the nest is done, she digs a deep hole in its center. Three weeks after mating, the female is ready to lay her eggs into this hole.

Females often build nests in shady places or under trees.

Alligator eggs usually begin hatching in August.

Eggs

The female lays 20 to 50 eggs in the nest. She uses one of her back feet to cushion the eggs as they fall into the nest. The eggs are about three inches (eight centimeters) long.

Once she is finished laying eggs, the female covers the nest with leaves and plants. This covers the eggs and keeps them warm. It also helps to hide the eggs from animals. Raccoons, snakes, and other animals eat alligator eggs that they find.

Female alligators do not sit on their nests. They swim or lay near them during the two months while the eggs incubate. Incubate means to keep eggs warm before they hatch. If anything comes too close to the nest, the females will hiss and may even attack.

The females take care of their eggs. They keep them cool with water. They do this by climbing out of the water and standing over the nests. Cool water drips off their bodies and onto the nests. Females make so many trips from the water that they wear paths to the nests. These paths are called alligator roads.

Hatchlings

Alligator eggs usually begin hatching in August. The young alligators begin to break out of their shells. They use their caruncles to crack open their shells. A caruncle is a small, sharp point at the end of a newborn alligator's snout. Young alligators are called hatchlings.

Hatchlings are about eight inches (20 centimeters) long when they hatch. They have yellow stripes on their backs. As they grow older, the young alligators lose the stripes.

If the female is around when her young hatch, she helps them out of the nest. She also leads them to the water. If not, hatchlings find their own way to the water. Hatchlings are on their own once they enter the water. Most female alligators leave their young once they are born. Hatchlings stay in groups called pods at least through their first winter.

For the first few days, hatchlings may return from the water to eat the left-over yolk from their eggs. After the yolk is gone, they must search for food.

Many hatchlings do not survive their first few weeks. Birds, snakes, and turtles eat many of them. Sometimes hatchlings make chirping sounds when they are in danger. Then the mother may come to protect them. The mother may do this until the next mating season. At that time, the young are about eight months old.

Growing

Hatchlings grow quickly during their first years. They grow about one foot (30 centimeters) per year during their first five years. Adult male alligators can reach lengths of up to 14 feet (four meters). Some alligators have weighed almost 1,000 pounds (450 kilograms).

Chapter 4

Past and Future

Alligators have always been respected by Native Americans. Native Americans told stories about the world around them. These stories are called myths. Creek people told this story about the alligator and the trickster rabbit.

How Rabbit Fooled Alligator

One day, Alligator was sunning himself on a log. Rabbit came along and decided to play a trick. Rabbit told Alligator that Devil believed Alligator was afraid of him. Alligator was mad. Alligator said that he was not afraid of Devil.

Rabbit dared Alligator to climb the hill where Devil lived. Rabbit warned Alligator not

In the myth, rabbit saw Alligator sunning himself on a log.

to be afraid of fire or smoke. Rabbit said these were signs that Devil was nearby. Alligator said that he was not afraid. He and Rabbit climbed the hill.

Rabbit started the grass near Alligator on fire. Rabbit told Alligator not to worry because the smoke was just Devil. Alligator did not run. The fire came closer and burned Alligator. Finally, Alligator could not stand the heat. He ran down the hill and jumped into the water.

Rabbit laughed at the trick he had pulled on Alligator. Alligator never trusted Rabbit or any of Rabbit's family again.

Dangers

The alligator comes from one of the oldest animal groups on earth. Scientists have seen alligators with part of their jaws torn off, their legs missing, or their backs broken. Yet these alligators survived and lived long lives. Many other animals would have died.

Alligators can survive many things. But by 1900, many alligators in the United States had died. People built houses on swampland where

alligators lived. Other land was drained of water and changed into farmland. Alligators were running out of places to live.

People killed nearly 5 million alligators in Florida and Louisiana between 1865 and 1960. Hunting was not controlled. People were allowed to kill as many alligators as they wanted. Hunters skinned the alligators. People made shoes, boots, purses, and handbags from the alligator skins.

Extinction
Alligator hunters killed too many alligators. By 1960, the American alligator was in danger of becoming extinct. Many people wanted to protect the alligator. In 1967, the federal government placed alligators on the endangered species list.

In 1973, the U.S. government passed the Endangered Species Act. This banned the hunting of alligators and other endangered animals. The number of wild alligators soon began to increase.

Today, scientists believe there are 3 million alligators in the southern United States. The U.S. Fish and Wildlife Service took alligators off the endangered species list in 1987.

The Alligator's Future
Because there are so many alligators in the wild, it is now legal to raise alligators on farms. Alligator farms sell the animals' meat and skin.

Scientists believe there are 3 million alligators in the United States today.

Today, the American alligator is not in danger of extinction, but its future is still uncertain. There is no guarantee the alligator population will stay large. People are building on land where alligators live. As human populations increase, the alligator's home is disappearing. But if land is set aside for the alligator, the oldest living reptile will continue to survive.

Long Tail

Words to Know

alligator road (AL-i-gay-tuhr ROHD)—the path worn from a den or nest to a gator hole
basking (BASK-ing)—to lie in the sun
bellow (BEL-oh)—a loud sound like a roar
caruncle (CAHR-uhng-kuhl)—a small, sharp point at the end of a newborn alligator's snout
cold-blooded (KOHLD BLUHD-id)—an animal that has a body temperature which changes depending on the weather
crocodilian (krah-keh-DIHL-ee-in)—reptiles that are grouped together by scientists
den (DEN)—a tunnel or room where an alligator lives
extinct (ek-STINGKT)—when something has died out and no longer exists
gator hole (GAY-tur HOHL)—a hole that an alligator digs for itself to live in
hatchling (HACH-ling)—an alligator that has just hatched from its egg

To Learn More

Arnosky, Jim. *All about Alligators*. New York: Scholastic, 1994.

Graham, Ada and Frank Graham. *Alligators*. New York: Delacorte Press, 1979.

May, Julian. *Alligator Hole*. Chicago: Follett Publishing, 1969.

Scott, Jack Denton. *Alligator*. New York: G.P. Putnam and Sons, 1984.

Staub, Frank. *Alligators*. Minneapolis: Lerner Publications, 1995.

Useful Addresses

Crocodilian Specialist Group
Florida Museum of Natural History
University of Florida
Gainesville, FL 32611-7800

**Florida Game and Fresh Water Fish
  Commission**
4005 South Main Street
Gainesville, FL 32601-9099

National Wildlife Federation
1400 16th Street NW
Washington, DC 20036-2217

U.S. Fish and Wildlife Service
1849 C Street NW
Washington, DC 20240

Internet Sites

The American Alligator
http://gnv.ifas.ufl.edu/www/agator/htm/aligator.
htm

**Crocodilians: Natural History &
Conservation**
http://www.flmnh.ufl.edu/natsci/herpetology/
brittoncrocs/cnhc.html

The Electronic Zoo: Reptile Page
http://netvet.wustl.edu/reptiles.htm

The Gator Hole
http://magicnet.net/~mgodwin

ZooNet
http://www.mindspring.com/~zoonet

Index